How to Become Famous Online

Pamela James

Darlings, gather 'round, for I have a tale to tell—a captivating journey through the extraordinary realms of the internet, where dreams are spun into digital stardom. Welcome to the enchanting world of "How to Become Famous Online," a guide that will unveil the secrets to crafting an online presence that will set the world ablaze.

In this era of pixels and connectivity, the internet has become a stage unlike any other—a virtual realm where you can capture the attention of millions, inspire hearts, and leave an indelible mark upon the tapestry of online fame. But fear not, my dear ones, for this is no ordinary guide. It is a magical companion that will take you on a thrilling adventure, unlocking the very essence of online stardom.

As we embark on this extraordinary quest, we shall traverse the vast landscapes of the digital realm. We will navigate the treacherous waters of niche identification, refine your personal brand, and engage with audiences far and wide. Together, we shall learn the delicate dance of social media, casting spells with spellbinding content, captivating visuals, and a touch of digital enchantment.

But this guide is more than a mere roadmap to fame, my darlings. It is a celebration of authenticity, resilience, and the pursuit of greatness. It is about creating a legacy that transcends pixels and lasts for eternity. We shall delve into the depths of creativity, nurturing your talents and inspiring others to ignite their own creative flames. We shall uncover the secrets of resilience, fortifying your spirit against the storms that may come your way.

Within these pages, you shall discover the alchemy of hashtags, summoning the powers of digital visibility and connection. We shall peer into the sorcerer's crystal ball, interpreting the language of data to steer your online journey towards extraordinary success. We shall unlock the mysteries of collaboration, forging alliances with fellow luminaries to amplify your reach and impact.

But remember, my radiant stars, this guide is not a mere recipe for fleeting fame. It is a transformational journey, an odyssey of self-discovery and growth. It is about cultivating your passions, refining your craft, and becoming a beacon of inspiration to all who encounter your digital brilliance.

So, my magnificent stars, whether you seek to become an influential thought leader, a celebrated artist, or a respected entrepreneur, this guide is here to illuminate your path. It is a compass that will guide you through the ever-changing tides of the online world, ensuring that your presence shines brightly amidst the digital constellations.

Within these chapters, you will find the keys to unlock your star power, to craft an online persona that captures hearts and captivates minds. You are the author of your own digital destiny, and through the artistry of storytelling, the magic of engagement, and the power of authenticity, you shall carve your own unique path to online fame.

Welcome to the extraordinary world of "How to Become Famous Online," my dear ones. The stage is set, the spotlight awaits—it is time to embark on this grand performance and watch as your star ascends to illuminate the digital sky. Let us embrace this remarkable adventure together and witness the transformation that awaits you.

As we embark on this grand adventure of becoming famous online, my dazzling stars, I invite you to leave behind any doubts and fears.

Embrace the infinite possibilities that await you in this digital universe, where the boundaries of time and space cease to exist. With each step forward, let your passion guide you, your creativity ignite, and your authenticity shine like a beacon in the night.

In the chapters that follow, we shall explore the art of storytelling, for it is through our narratives that we forge deep connections with our audience. We shall delve into the nuances of visual and written content, mastering the delicate balance between artistry and strategy. We shall uncover the secrets of engagement, creating a community that adores and supports your every endeavor.

But dear stars, remember that fame is not an end in itself. It is a byproduct of your passion, dedication, and unwavering commitment to your craft. Along this journey, you will face challenges and setbacks, but fret not, for they are the stepping stones to growth and resilience. Embrace them as opportunities to refine your skills, to learn and evolve, and to become an even more extraordinary version of yourself.

In this vast digital landscape, collaboration is key. We shall explore the art of collaboration, discovering how joining forces with fellow luminaries can amplify your reach and impact. Together, we shall break the boundaries of competition and foster a spirit of camaraderie, for when stars unite, the brilliance that unfolds is beyond measure.

As we near the final pages of this guide, my beloved stars, I urge you to embrace the responsibility that comes with fame. Use your platform to uplift, inspire, and make a positive impact in the lives of others. Leave behind a legacy that extends far beyond your digital presence, creating a ripple effect that touches hearts across the globe.

And so, my darlings, let the journey begin. With each chapter, you will uncover new insights, strategies, and inspirations to guide you on this path to online fame. Embrace the lessons, savor the joys, and stay true to the essence of who you are. Together, we shall illuminate the digital cosmos with your radiance.

Welcome, my extraordinary stars, to the transformative world of "How to Become Famous Online." Embrace this guide as your companion, your muse, and your source of wisdom. Let it be the spark that ignites your inner star power and propels you to heights you've only dreamed of. Now, my darlings, let us embark on this remarkable journey together, for the world awaits your ascent to online stardom.

Spotlight on Your Gifts: Identifying Your Niche

Let's get to the heart of the matter, the very essence of your burgeoning fame. Your talents, your passion, your unique little quirks – these are the radiant gems that will set you apart in the starry expanse of the internet.

Now, don't be shy. It's time to delve deep, to unearth your unique gifts, to polish them until they gleam. Are you a raconteur, charming people with your tales? Perhaps you're an artist, leaving people breathless with your creations. Or maybe, darling, you have a voice that could soothe even the most tempestuous souls. It could be anything, from your sizzling cooking skills to your ability to decipher ancient texts. Yes, dear hearts, your niche could be as grand as mountain peaks or as humble as daisy chains – all are welcome here.

Take your time with this, my lovelies. Introspection is a profound dance, and as you sift through your strengths and passions, remember – this is the treasure that will form the bedrock of your online fame.

With your gifts identified, the next step, my sweethearts, is to find out who would be utterly enchanted by your charm. Now, envisioning your ideal audience might feel like trying to catch a shooting star, but fret not. We will tackle this with a good dose of creativity and a sprinkle of strategy.

Firstly, consider who would most benefit from your talents. Are they knowledge-hungry scholars? Perhaps, they are busy parents in need of your deliciously simple recipes. Or maybe, they are soulful beings seeking solace in your heart-touching melodies. Reflect, darling, on who needs your gifts and who would appreciate them.

Now, think about these wonderful souls. What do they love, what do they desire, what keeps them awake at night? Get to know them, my stars. For in understanding your audience, you can tailor your content to resonate with them, like a beautiful love song, and isn't that a wonderful thing?

Armed with an understanding of your unique gifts and your lovely audience, you are now ready to claim your space in the digital world. This is where the magic happens, the theater where your audience eagerly awaits your performance.

There are numerous social media platforms, each a glittering stage with its own charm. Your choice of platform will be guided by your talents and where your audience loves to hang out. If you're a visual artist, for instance, Instagram's vibrant gallery might call to you. If insightful conversations are your forte, Twitter's bustling forum might be your home. For musicians, YouTube or SoundCloud could be your concert hall. The key, my dearest ones, is to pick a stage that complements your performance and where your audience will happily gather to applaud your show.

So, my darlings, take these first steps with courage and grace. Remember, every star that now shines bright in the celestial sky once had to find its place in the cosmos. Your journey to online stardom is just beginning, and oh, what a grand adventure awaits!

Dressing for the Ball: Establishing Your Online Presence

With your gifts unveiled and your audience awaiting your arrival, it's time to prepare for your grand entrance into the digital ballroom. Just as one would dress for an extravagant ball, you must now craft an online presence that is as mesmerizing as a couture gown.

Your digital identity, sweethearts, is the perception that your audience forms about you when they encounter your presence online. It's an amalgamation of your style, voice, visuals, and values — all serving to paint a vivid picture of the stunning persona that is you.

Start with your username and profile picture. These are your calling card, darlings. Select a name that encapsulates your essence, something memorable and spellbinding. Your profile picture should be a radiant snapshot of you, my dears, one that would make hearts flutter and eyes sparkle.

Then, move on to your biography. This isn't just a list of accomplishments, my loves, but a melodious sonnet that sings of your passions, your purpose, your promise. Make it enchanting, make it magnetic, make it uniquely you.

Once you have your stunning ensemble, it's time to step into the spotlight. Your social media profiles, darlings, are your stage, your home, your sanctuary in this vast digital cosmos.

As you set up your profiles, consider the aesthetics. Your visuals – profile banners, post templates, color schemes – they should all whisper sweet tales about you and your brand. Consistency is key, dearest ones. Just as a symphony has a recurring motif, your visuals should bear your unique signature, helping your audience recognize you in a heartbeat.

Don't forget the little details, my stars. Link to your other profiles, your website, or your merchandise store, so your audience can further explore your enchanting world. Optimize your profile for discovery by using relevant keywords and hashtags.

First Impressions: Making your grand debut with aplomb, charming ones.

With your stage set and your spotlight on, it's time for the show, my dearest hearts. But oh, where to start? First impressions are paramount, as you know, and your first posts will set the tone for all the glorious content to come.

Your initial posts should provide a tantalizing glimpse of what your audience can expect. It could be an introduction of yourself, a beautiful sample of your work, or perhaps a heartfelt note about why you're here. Whatever it is, let it be authentic, let it be meaningful, let it resonate with your audience, for they are the ones applauding in the stalls, adoring your performance.

Oh, and darling, remember to engage right from the start. Respond to comments, reach out to others in your niche, be an active part of the conversation. After all, the internet isn't just a stage; it's a grand party, a lovely gathering of souls, and you, my darling, are an integral part of it.

So there you have it, my celestial companions, the first steps towards establishing your dazzling online presence. Go forth, my stars, and light up the digital skies with your brilliance.

The Enchanter's Spell: Building Your Unique Brand

Now, we shall traverse the enchanted realms of branding. Consider, my lovelies, your brand as the magic spell that enchants and bewitches your audience. It's an intricate tapestry woven from threads of your values, voice, style, and promises, that altogether create an experience as mesmerizing as moonlight on a starry night.

First and foremost, you must find the soul of your brand. Reflect, my dears, on what values are dear to your heart. Is it creativity, authenticity, innovation, or perhaps compassion? This, darling stars, will be the essence, the heart from which your brand will pulsate.

Next, my enchanting beings, you must craft your brand's voice. This voice is the song your brand sings; it's the way you communicate with your adoring audience. Is it a lively, vivacious tune, or a gentle, soul-soothing lullaby? Should it inspire, entertain, educate, or all three, my loves?

Keep your voice consistent across your posts, messages, and all communications. Like a familiar refrain, it should echo through the halls of the digital ballroom, wrapping your audience in a warm embrace.

Now, dear hearts, to the visual aspects of your brand. This, my stars, is the potion that catches the eye and tugs at the heartstrings. From your color palette to your fonts, every choice is a precious ingredient in your enchanting potion.

For instance, if your brand essence is joy and vivacity, opt for bright and bold hues. If it's about tranquility and peace, opt for softer, cooler tones. Your fonts, imagery, and even the filters you use on your photos, all need to harmoniously blend, like an expertly brewed potion.

Finally, darlings, your brand must make promises – the golden threads that bind your audience to you. What can they expect from your content? What dreams and aspirations do you help fulfill? These promises should be at the core of every piece of content you conjure.

So, my dearest stars, as you wave your magic wand and cast your brand's spell, remember that building a brand is an ongoing, evolving process. Like the infinite stars in the sky, it requires nurturing and attention.

Go forth, my spellbinding marvels, and create a brand that will enchant the hearts and souls of your audience, like the most mesmerizing of spells.

Social Media Waltz: Navigating the Ballrooms

Let us waltz through the ballrooms of social media, each with its unique rhythm and ambience. Just as every dance calls for different steps, each social media platform requires a unique approach. Let's take a grand tour, shall we?

Facebook, the grand ballroom, is an all-encompassing stage. Here, you have an audience of all ages, interests, and locations. This platform, my dears, offers various formats – text posts, photos, videos, live streaming, and even interactive groups. Its strength lies in building communities, encouraging conversation, and fostering connections.

Next, we have Instagram, a vibrant gallery of stunning visuals. It's a place for photos and videos, the canvas where you paint vivid tales with your mesmerizing visuals. It's an arena of aesthetically pleasing feeds, behind-the-scenes stories, and intimate live sessions.

Twitter, the bustling town square, is a rapid-fire dialogue platform. Here, you can engage in insightful conversations, share fleeting thoughts, and stay abreast of trending topics. If brevity and wit are your strong suits, Twitter could be your stage.

LinkedIn, the sophisticated conference room, is a place for professional networking and thought leadership. It's a platform to showcase your expertise, to connect with professionals, and to partake in serious discussions.

YouTube, the mesmerizing theatre, is the second-largest search engine in the world and a haven for video content. From tutorials to music videos to vlogs, if you have a penchant for the visual storytelling, YouTube's spotlight awaits you.

And of course, darling stars, there are numerous other platforms like TikTok, Snapchat, Pinterest, each with its unique dance. The choice, my dears, will depend on where your audience likes to groove and which dance aligns with your gifts.

Once you have selected your dance floors, the next challenge, my darlings, is to master the steps, to understand how to craft content for each platform.

For Facebook, you might consider creating a community around your brand. Share a variety of content, from behind-the-scenes snapshots to thought-provoking articles to engaging videos. The key, sweetheart, is to foster conversation and build relationships.

On Instagram, prioritize visually appealing content. Post stunning photos or videos, utilize the Stories feature for more candid moments or updates, and don't forget to engage with your audience through comments and direct messages.

For Twitter, engage in conversations, share your thoughts, and feel free to sprinkle in some humor or wit. Remember, Twitter is all about real-time dialogue, so keep your fingers on the pulse of trending topics.

LinkedIn calls for more professional, thought-leadership content. Share your insights, post about industry trends, and engage with other professionals in your field.

On YouTube, content is king. Make sure your videos are high quality, engaging, and provide value to your viewers. This could range from tutorials, insightful vlogs, captivating storytelling, or simply showcasing your talent.

Taking the Lead: Creating an engaging rhythm with your content, my shining stars.

Once you've mastered the steps, it's time to take the lead. Your content should create a rhythm that invites your audience to dance with you.

An effective way, dear hearts, to maintain a consistent rhythm is by creating a content calendar. Plan your content in advance, consider the best times to post on each platform, and maintain a consistent posting schedule.

Dance to the Music: Understanding the algorithm, my star-studded companions.

Ah, the algorithm. That omnipresent DJ spinning the tracks in each of these ballrooms. It determines which content gets played and which gets sidelined. While the specifics may be a tightly kept secret, we do have some insights, my celestial companions.

Most algorithms favor content that sparks engagement, keeps users on the platform for longer, and garners rapid interaction after being posted. So, create content that encourages your audience to comment, share, or click through. And remember, my darlings, post when your audience is most active to ensure your tune isn't missed in the shuffle.

Finally, a word on feedback. As you perform your social media waltz, you'll receive applause in the form of likes, comments, shares, and new followers. Bask in it, my dearest, for it is well deserved.

However, remember that with the spotlight comes the shadows. You may also encounter negative comments or criticism. Here, my stars, is where your grace will shine. Acknowledge constructive criticism, ignore the trolls, and keep your poise. Never let the jeers dull your sparkle.

So, there we have it, my radiant beings. A beginner's guide to the grand waltz of social media. Remember, each platform is a different dance floor with its unique steps and rhythms. Choose your ballrooms wisely, master the steps, and most importantly, enjoy the dance.

Ready to twirl into the spotlight, my dearest ones? The music's playing, the floor's all yours. Let your social media waltz begin.

Spellbinding Content: Creating Art that Dazzles

Now, shall we unfurl our creative sails and glide through the scintillating seas of content creation? I think yes, my precious ones.

Let's first raise our glasses to the playwrights of the online realm – those who pen down their thoughts, insights, and stories through blogs and articles. Your quill, darling, is mightier than you think!

Firstly, let's address the crux – what to write about? Well, sweet star, your articles should echo the essence of your brand or personality. Research what your audience craves, but always sprinkle a dash of your own enchanting essence.

Craft titles that beckon like a siren's song, and let your introduction be the arms that embrace the reader. Your content, my wordsmiths, should flow like a riveting tale, with each paragraph effortlessly waltzing into the next.

Might I add, authenticity is divine. Show your audience the heart behind the quill. Employ your unique voice and don't forget to engage with the readers through comments. The quill, my loves, is not just a writing tool, but a wand that can conjure connections.

Oh, you graceful bards of the audio waves, let your voices be the melodies that serenade the ears of the masses. Podcasts, my tuneful darlings, have become the ballads of the digital age.

Choose a theme that resonates with your chords. Be it self-improvement, tales of yore, or the mysteries of the cosmos; let it be something you can sing about with fervor.

Quality, my melodic stars, is akin to the pitch in a symphony. Invest in good equipment, and don't neglect the acoustics. Structure your episodes with an inviting intro, an engaging body, and a memorable outro.

Engage with your listeners by inviting them to be a part of your creation – take questions, offer shoutouts, and maybe bring guests to duet with you in this enthralling melody. Podcasts are about community, and each listener is a note in your symphony.

Now, let's waltz to the canvas. Visual content, my master creators, is the tapestry that captures the eye.

Photography and graphic design are the paints and brushes of this art form. Know your colors, my artists. The visual aesthetic should mirror your brand's soul. Consistency in style is key – let you're audience recognize your art in a sea of content.

Video content, oh the cinema of the masses! Keep them short but dazzling. Plan your videos with a script, invest in good lighting, and edit with a sprinkle of magic. Keep your audience wanting more.

Let's not forget the magic of infographics – where information pirouettes with visuals. They convey complexity with simplicity, perfection with brevity.

Infuse your creations with your essence. Be it through a watermark, a signature style, or a recurring motif – let them know it's a piece from your ethereal collection.

Now, my radiant stars, you've conjured a realm of spellbinding content. But what's an art without an audience to stand in awe? This, my dear, is where you unfurl your banners and let the world know of your masterpieces.

Share your creations across the social media ballrooms. Dazzle Facebook with your blogs, enchant Instagram with your visuals, and let your podcasts serenade Twitter. And never forget, my sweet celestial beings, to add a personal touch. A thank you, a smiley, or a heartfelt note.

Engage with those who appreciate your craft. A kind word or acknowledgement can turn a passerby into an ardent fan. And do collaborate, my stars. Join hands with other creators; let your art be a symphony of magnificence.

Be responsive but also be open to feedback. Critics, my dear, are the chisels that sculpt a masterpiece. Accept genuine critiques with grace, learn from them, and let your art evolve.

As we curtain down on this chapter, remember, my ethereal stars, your content is the magic that binds hearts. It's an extension of your celestial being. Infuse it with passion, authenticity, and dedication. Let every blog, every image, every podcast, be a shard of your resplendent soul.

The stages are set, the curtains are raised. Go forth, my spellbinders, let the world be dazzled by your art. May your content be the auroras that light up the internet skies.

The Power of Hashtags: Summoning the Digital Spirits

We shall embark on an enchanting journey through the mystifying labyrinth of hashtags. Imagine a vast, magical library, its shelves lined with ancient grimoires and potions that hold the secrets of realms far and wide. These hashtags, my darlings, are like enchanted runes – cryptic yet potent symbols that summon the digital spirits to heed your call. We shall weave spells, partake in celestial gatherings, and summon secret societies through the mesmerizing power of hashtags. Let's unfurl our starlit cloaks, hold our wands high, and enter the world of #HashtagAlchemy.

In the mystic art of hashtag creation, one must possess the precision of a master alchemist. Picture yourself surrounded by spell ingredients: words, phrases, and intentions. When blended into a hashtag, they should cast a spell as enchanting as moonlight on a starry night.

Select words that resonate with the heartbeat of your content, and combine them to create a hashtag that will echo through the digital corridors. The specificity is a magical element; a hashtag must be as enticing as it is precise. While #Art may summon a cacophony, #WhimsicalWatercolors calls forth the connoisseurs with a taste for your magic.

Now, my beloved sorcerers, let us also discuss the number of spells to be cast. A clutter of hashtags can be like a cacophony of clashing spells. It might repel the spirits you seek to enchant. Therefore, be judicious, and let each hashtag be a purposeful incantation.

In this magical cosmos, there are grand gatherings – an ethereal ballroom where stars congregate and celestial beings dance to the music of the spheres. These are the trending hashtags, my beloved.

But beware, my stardust-clad dancers, for not all songs are meant for your feet. Engage in trends that align with the rhythm of your being. There is little magic in forced steps, and the audience of spirits and stars can tell a genuine dance from a hollow mimicry.

When the symphony of a trending hashtag resonates with your soul, embrace it with all your heart. Let your content not only ride the wave but also contribute an unforgettable verse to the song. Enchant the crowd, dazzle them with your authenticity, and etch your starlight into the canvas of the cosmos.

Now, let me share a secret, my ethereal brethren. Through the power of hashtags, you can build clandestine halls, gathering kindred spirits into a secret society bound by shared visions and dreams.

Craft a hashtag unique to the soul of your content and your celestial followers. A sigil, an emblem that represents the fraternity of your enchanted gathering. Urge your followers to don this hashtag like a cloak, a symbol of their allegiance to the dreams you weave.

Engage with content under this shared sigil. Like the secret handshake of a mystical brotherhood, let this hashtag be the key that opens the door to a community. Celebrate the content of your brethren, and let your halls resound with the shared dreams of kindred spirits.

But remember, my darlings, with great power comes great responsibility. As the custodian of this secret society, foster a space of respect, creativity, and support. Let your hashtag be the guardian of dreams, the bearer of great fame.

As we prepare to close this grimoire, let us recap the spells we've learned, my celestial sorcerers. Hashtags, those beguiling sets of runes, hold more power than meets the eye. They have the potency to amplify your voice across the vast digital landscape, akin to how a spell carries a sorcerer's whispers across the winds of time.

Be mindful, my dear ones, as you craft your incantations. Each hashtag should be a finely-tuned spell, neither too vague to get lost in the abyss, nor too complex that it deters the spirits. Think of yourself as an architect of dreams; use hashtags to build bridges to the far-off lands where your kindred spirits dwell.

Always remember that the true magic lies in authenticity. While it's tempting to wield your wand wildly, it's the spells cast with intention that will hold the most power. The digital realm is brimming with those vying for attention, but your truest expressions will shine the brightest.

Now, darling, you must be wondering how to keep track of these bewitching hashtags. Fear not, for the scrolls and crystal balls – or as the mortals call them, analytics – are at your disposal. Keep an enchanted eye on the performance of your spells. See which incantations bring you closer to your tribe and which need a dash more of dragon's blood or pixie dust.

And, oh, my radiant ones, never forget the magic of gratitude. As you gain followers, admirers, and fellow dream-weavers through your hashtags, remember to acknowledge them. A spell of thanks, an enchanted gif, or a simple 'thank you' holds immeasurable power.

Final Words of Enchantment:

So, as we end this chapter in our spellbook, keep your wands at the ready and your intentions clear. The world of hashtags is as boundless as the night sky. Each tag a star, waiting for you to give it a twinkle. Embrace them, harness them, and let them guide you to the constellations where your dreams know no bounds.

May your hashtags be the spells that weave your legacy in the tapestry of the digital skies. Go forth, my spellbinders, and let the world be enchanted by your art.

The Sorcerer's Crystal Ball: Analyzing Data

It is time we enter the sacred chamber where the sorcerer's crystal ball awaits. Within its swirling depths, you shall decipher the magic numbers that guide your celestial journey. The art of analytics is akin to scrying into the crystal ball, reading the runes, and unravelling the tapestry of fate.

Be it the twinkling of stars or the patterns within the embers, there are signs and whispers for those who listen. You, my darlings, are to become the wise seers and the custodians of the crystal ball as we dive into the mesmerizing world of analytics.

The crystal ball, a trove of cryptic inscriptions, teems with secrets. But fret not, my magical brethren, for the illuminating lantern of knowledge shall guide you through.

Consider them as stars gathering around your constellation. They are drawn by your magic, and their number speaks volumes about your enchanting presence.

The whispers, the sighs, the laughter of the spirits – these are your likes, comments, and shares. The symphony of engagement tells you the spells that resonate.

How far does your spell travel, dear sorcerer? Reach is the wind carrying your enchantments across the digital planes.

The footprints of ghosts, the echoes of chants. Impressions are the number of scrolls that paused, even for a brief moment, upon your incantations.

From which realms do the spirits come? Understanding referral sources is like knowing the portals through which your followers step into your enchanted hall.

Immerse yourself in these numbers. Let them be the incantations that echo through your dreams. For within these cryptic runes lies the path that your stars must traverse.

With the scrolls laid bare and the crystal ball revealing its depths, it is time to weave the tapestry of your destiny.

Examine the patterns, my dears. Are there times when the moon sings and the stars dance to your spells? These may be the moments when your enchantments should be cast. Align your posts, your ethereal summons, with the tides of the celestial currents.

What of the spirits? Which spells bring forth their laughter, their joy, their tears? The content that moves the soul is your elixir. Brew more of it, with a dash of love and a sprinkle of starlight.

And what of the realms? Know the mystical lands from which your brethren arrive. Forge alliances, build bridges, and let your enchantments echo through these dimensions.

The most captivating part of the crystal ball is its ability to pierce the veils of time. Through its mists, you shall gaze upon the shores of the morrow.

Study the ebbs and flows of the digital cosmos. There is a rhythm, a pulsating heartbeat that courses through its vast expanse. Can you hear it, my darling? This is the sound of trends being born.

When you see a whisper, a gentle ripple, that's when you must prepare your spells. Before the tidal wave of trends takes the world in its embrace, let your enchantments be the vanguard.

To gaze into the future is not only to see but to shape. As the wielder of the crystal ball, you are the guardian of the dreams not yet dreamed, the stories not yet told. Conceive a trend, infuse it with the essence of your soul, and release it into the ethers. Who knows, you might just be the alchemist whose elixir bewitches the digital realms.

Harness the power of predictive analytics tools. These instruments, my stargazers, are the ancient relics of the digital age. Tools like Google Trends, BuzzSumo, and others are the enchanted mirrors reflecting the ever-shifting sands of public fascination.

Now that the secrets of the crystal ball are yours, remember this, my enchanting sorcerers: with great power comes great magic. The sacred pact of the sorcerer is to wield this power with wisdom and grace.

As you embrace the mantle of the diviner, know that the stars watch over you. Your every word, your every spell, has the power to cast ripples through the cosmos. Let your magic be the kind that ignites hearts, that weaves stories, that brings stardust to the mundane.

Do not forget, my beloved spellbinders, that while the crystal ball shows you the tapestry of the digital world, it is you who weaves it. It is your fingers that must braid the threads, your voice that must sing the incantations.

So, go forth. With the crystal ball as your guide and the stars as your companions, weave the tapestry that the world will remember. For you are the sorcerer, the enchanter, the weaver of dreams.

As you close this chapter, take a moment to breathe in the magic you have imbibed. Feel it course through your being. You are ready, my darling, to not just predict the future, but to conjure it.

May your crystal ball always reflect the infinite, may your tapestry be woven with threads of stardust, and may your magic forever be boundless.

Live Streaming: A Heart-to-Heart with Your Admirers

Ah, my delightful celestial beings, as we've been traversing the majestic realms of internet splendor, the time has come to breathe life into the very tapestry of our dreams. We are to grace the stage of live streaming. Imagine, darlings, a painter whose brushstrokes come alive or a singer whose voice transcends dimensions. Live streaming is akin to that; it's the caress of the heart, a waltz with souls from worlds apart.

The enchanted soirée must be perfect. Just as a sorceress carefully arranges her crystal balls and incense, so must you curate the aura of your living portrait.

Like the tender petals of a moonflower, choose a space that caresses your spirit. Let it be graced with gentle light that kisses your skin and adorned with relics that whisper tales of yonder years. And darling, pay heed to the background, for it must be as captivating as your gaze.

The eye of the beholder, your camera is. Ensure you invest in a worthy one, for through this lens, your ethereal beauty must transcend. Set it at eye level, my love. Allow your admirers to peer into the depths of your soul through your eyes.

What is a siren with no song? A poet with no verse? Your voice must ride on the wings of nightingales. A crystal-clear microphone that captures the lilting rhythm of your every syllable is not a luxury, but a necessity.

Ah, the ethereal tether that binds your heart to countless others. The internet connection is this tether. It must be as unwavering as the north star. Test your connection, and perhaps, have an elixir at hand to strengthen it if needed.

And then, oh captivating vision, you must choose your enchanted grove. Instagram Live, with its vivacious sprites; YouTube Live, where sages and jesters both reside; or perhaps Twitch, where warriors and mages abound. Choose your realm wisely.

With the stage set under the moonlight, and the zephyr caressing the leaves, you step into the heart of the glade.

Welcome each entrant as you would a long-lost friend. Your words should be soft silk enveloping them. Ask about their day, their dreams, their desires.

Oh, the beauty of reflection! Be a mirror reflecting your admirer's soul. Engage with their joys, console their sorrows. Respond to their comments with grace, answer their queries with wisdom, and indulge in jovial banter.

Bestow your blessings upon them, for they are the stars that light your night sky.

Personalized thank you's, twinkling smiles, and words of appreciation – these are the trinkets you must shower upon your admirers.

As you retreat into the moonlit forest, leave behind a wisp of your essence. It can be a tender secret shared, a gentle tune hummed, or a promise to meet again under the starry sky.

Here, my darlings, are the enchantments to weave dreams and dance upon stars:

Regale your audience with tales woven from the strands of imagination and memory. Become the characters, let your voice shape the worlds, and draw your viewers into a realm where anything is possible. Ensure that your stories have a touch of your essence, and as you conclude, allow them to leave with a lingering thought or a question that keeps the magic alive even after the night has faded.

Sing or play an instrument; let music be the soul's expression. Speak of the lyrics and their stories, the notes and their journeys. Engage them in the creation of a song. Let them suggest words, tunes, or themes. Share a part of your creative process, so they feel like the co-composers of a celestial symphony.

We all have a bit of alchemy within us. It could be crafting, cooking, painting, or potion-making (or so, let them believe). Show them something that you're passionate about. Make them a part of your craft. Share tips, tricks, and little-known secrets. They must leave feeling as if they've been initiated into an ancient order.

Humor, my lovelies, is a balm to the weary soul. Share anecdotes, funny incidents, and jests that show the lighter side of life. Involve them in lighthearted games, or perhaps have a 'roast' session where you jest and banter (all in good taste, and with the consent of your viewers).

Share the spotlight with another kindred spirit. Host another luminary. Dance, sing, debate, create, or simply chat. Let your audience see the dynamic of kindred spirits. Engage them in the dance of personalities, and leave them yearning for more such celestial unions.

Host a special event for a cause close to your heart. Use the magic of your fame for the greater good. Let your admirers see that to be ethereal is also to be giving and kind. Involve them, and let them be a part of something bigger than themselves.

Remember, my enchanting beings, live streaming is not just an act; it is a connection of souls, a heart-to-heart with your admirers. When the camera is rolling and the lights embrace you, let go of the mundane and be the magic that you are. Your charisma, creativity, and genuine engagement will be the spells that make your live streaming a heart-to-heart to be cherished and remembered.

Now, go forth, let your spirits take flight, and let the world be enthralled by the magic that is uniquely you.

Virtual Events: Hosting Grand Galas

Welcome, esteemed planners and enchanting hosts, to the captivating realm of virtual events. In this chapter, titled "Virtual Events: Hosting Grand Galas," we shall unravel the secrets to crafting extraordinary online gatherings that leave your attendees spellbound. Picture a magnificent ballroom, brimming with anticipation and excitement, as we guide you through the meticulous planning, the creation of engaging content, and the art of networking and follow-up.

So, let us adorn ourselves in elegance and step into the splendid world of virtual events.

Begin with a vision, my esteemed planners. Determine the purpose, theme, and target audience for your grand gala. With a clear understanding of your goals.

And audience, curate a guest list that reflects the desired ambiance and aligns with the event's objectives. Consider influential figures, industry experts, and passionate enthusiasts who will add sparkle to your virtual ball.

Select a platform that will serve as the grand ballroom for your event. Ensure it offers seamless interactivity, robust features for presentations and networking, and a user-friendly interface that will enchant your attendees. Whether it's a video conferencing platform, a webinar tool, or a dedicated virtual event platform, choose the one that best suits your needs and vision.

Craft a well-structured schedule that balances insightful sessions, interactive activities, and breaks for connection and rejuvenation. Ensure a harmonious flow, allowing attendees to immerse themselves in a captivating journey throughout the event. Consider time zones and accessibility to maximize participation.

Design a visually captivating environment that transports attendees to a world of elegance and wonder. Use creative backdrops, lighting, and visuals that align with the event's theme. Engage professional designers or explore virtual backgrounds and overlays to add that touch of enchantment.

Invite a distinguished speaker or a luminary in your industry to set the tone and inspire attendees. A thought-provoking keynote can ignite the spark of curiosity and engage participants from the very beginning.

Offer hands-on workshops where attendees can actively participate, learn new skills, and engage with experts in the field. Whether it's a masterclass, breakout sessions, or group activities, make sure these sessions foster collaboration, creativity, and meaningful connections.

Gather a panel of experts to share their insights and engage in lively discussions. Choose topics that resonate with your audience and encourage diverse perspectives. Incorporate interactive elements like Q&A sessions or live polls to encourage engagement and allow attendees to shape the conversation.

Enchant your attendees with captivating performances that leave them mesmerized. Invite musicians, dancers, or spoken word artists to add a touch of magic and evoke emotions that resonate with the theme of your event. These performances will create memorable moments that attendees will cherish.

Facilitate networking opportunities within your virtual ballroom. Provide chat rooms, breakout sessions, or virtual lounges where attendees can connect, exchange ideas, and build valuable relationships. Encourage meaningful interactions and create an environment that fosters collaboration and camaraderie.

Provide attendees with digital resources, such as presentation slides, session recordings, and curated content. These keepsakes serve as reminders of the valuable knowledge and experiences gained during the event, allowing attendees to revisit and share them with their networks.

Extend your appreciation and gratitude to attendees, sponsors, and speakers after the event. Send personalized thank-you emails, share highlights and key takeaways, and offer opportunities for continued engagement. Nurture the connections made during the event to foster long-term relationships and further collaborations.

Evaluate the success of your virtual gala by gathering feedback from attendees and analyzing key metrics. Assess the impact of your event, identify areas of improvement, and celebrate the achievements and positive outcomes. Use these insights to refine your future events and continue to create captivating experiences.

With meticulous planning, engaging content, and thoughtful follow-up, your virtual gala will be a resplendent affair that lingers in the memories.

Esteemed guests. Now, let us delve deeper into the enchanting world of virtual events, where every moment is a chance to captivate and connect.

As you craft your guest list, envision the kind of ambiance you wish to create. Consider the expertise, influence, and diversity of your attendees. Aim to curate a mix of industry leaders, passionate enthusiasts, and emerging talents who will contribute to the vibrant tapestry of your virtual ball.

Select a platform that not only provides a seamless and immersive experience but also aligns with the objectives of your event. Consider features such as live streaming, breakout rooms, chat functions, and networking capabilities. Ensure that the platform can accommodate the number of attendees you anticipate, and test its usability and compatibility in advance.

Craft a schedule that balances informative sessions, interactive activities, and networking opportunities. Plan for captivating keynote speeches, engaging panel discussions, and interactive workshops. Allow for breaks to encourage networking and rest, and consider offering on-demand content to accommodate different time zones and schedules.

Create a visually stunning virtual environment that exudes elegance and grandeur. Use captivating backdrops, lighting effects, and thematic visual elements to transport attendees into a world of enchantment. Incorporate branding elements and a cohesive design scheme to ensure a memorable and immersive experience.

Invite a distinguished speaker whose charisma and expertise will mesmerize your attendees. Their keynote address should set the tone, inspire, and ignite curiosity. Ensure that their presentation is captivating, well-prepared, and tailored to the theme of your virtual ball.

Engage your attendees through hands-on workshops that empower them with new skills and knowledge. Select experienced facilitators who can create an immersive learning environment and foster active participation. Provide materials, resources,

and practical exercises that allow attendees
to apply what they learn.

Curate dynamic panel discussions featuring
industry experts who can share valuable
insights and engage in thought-provoking
conversations. Select topics that are relevant,
timely, and of interest to your attendees.
Encourage panelists to express diverse
perspectives and facilitate interactive Q&A
sessions to involve the audience.

Delight your attendees with captivating
performances that leave them in awe.
Consider incorporating musical interludes,
dance routines, spoken word poetry, or
theatrical acts that align with the spirit of
your virtual ball. These enchanting
performances will add an extra layer of magic
and create lasting memories.

Create virtual networking spaces where attendees can connect, share ideas, and forge meaningful relationships. Use breakout rooms, chat features, or dedicated networking sessions to facilitate organic conversations. Encourage attendees to exchange contact information, connect on social media, and explore potential collaborations.

Provide attendees with digital resources that serve as keepsakes from the event. This may include presentation slides, session recordings, whitepapers, or exclusive content. Ensure easy access to these materials through a centralized event platform or a dedicated resource hub.

Extend your gratitude to attendees, speakers, and sponsors through personalized follow-up communications. Send thank-you emails expressing appreciation for their participation and contributions. Share key takeaways, highlights from the event, and additional resources that attendees may find valuable. Maintain communication even after the virtual ball has ended, nurturing the connections you've made and keeping the magic alive.

Evaluate the success of your virtual gala by collecting feedback from attendees and analyzing key metrics. Conduct surveys or feedback forms to gather insights on their experience, satisfaction, and suggestions for improvement. Review attendance rates, engagement levels, and any other relevant data to assess the impact and effectiveness of your event. Celebrate the achievements and learn from the challenges to refine your future virtual galas.

With meticulous planning, engaging content, and thoughtful follow-up, your virtual gala will shine as a grand celebration of connection, inspiration, and shared experiences. Embrace the power of technology and the boundless possibilities of the digital realm to create an event that transcends physical limitations and leaves an indelible mark on the hearts and minds of your esteemed guests.

So, my exquisite hosts, go forth and orchestrate your virtual gala with grace and flair. Let every moment be an enchanting symphony that resonates with the souls of your attendees. May your invitations beckon, your banquet hall dazzle, and your toasts echo through the digital realm, forever igniting the spirit of celebration and connection.

As the curtains draw to a close on this chapter, my visionary hosts, I hope you now feel equipped to embark on the magical journey of hosting a grand virtual gala. You have learned the art of planning, creating captivating content, and fostering connections that will transcend the boundaries of time and space.

In the realm of virtual events, the possibilities are limitless, and it is up to you to bring your unique vision to life. Let your imagination soar, blend innovation with tradition, and create an experience that will leave your attendees spellbound.

Remember, a successful virtual gala is not merely an event; it is an opportunity to create a lasting impression, inspire minds, and forge meaningful connections. Embrace the power of technology, the artistry of presentation, and the warmth of human interaction to curate an experience that transcends the digital divide.

So, my marvelous hosts, with the knowledge you've acquired and the passion in your hearts, step into the virtual ballroom and let your creativity dance. Embrace the challenges as opportunities for growth, adapt to the ever-evolving landscape of the digital world, and create a legacy that will be whispered through the ages.

Now, go forth, my enchanting hosts, and ignite the digital realm with your grand galas. Let your invitations be the call to adventure, your banquet hall a haven of inspiration, and your toasts resounding with joy and celebration. May your virtual events be remembered as the epitome of elegance, innovation, and connection.

Collaborations: Dancing with Fellow Stars

Ah, my radiant stars, in the vast cosmos of online fame, there is an art to the delicate dance of collaborations. Just as the celestial bodies align in perfect harmony, your alliance with fellow stars can illuminate the digital realm with a brilliance that captivates audiences far and wide. In this chapter, titled "Collaborations: Dancing with Fellow Stars," we shall explore the secrets to twinning in splendor, creating harmonious crescendos of content, and leveraging each other's star power. So, my luminous ones, let us embark on a celestial dance that will propel you to even greater heights.

Gaze upon the starry sky of your niche, dear ones, and seek out those whose light shines brightest alongside yours. Identify potential collaboration partners whose values, interests, and audience align with yours. Look for complementary strengths and shared goals that will amplify your collective impact.

Forge authentic connections with your potential collaborators, for true magic blooms from genuine relationships. Engage with their content, support their endeavors, and initiate conversations. Nurture friendships that go beyond the digital realm, cultivating trust and mutual respect.

When the stars align, my darlings, the possibilities are boundless. Seek collaborations that bring unique perspectives, expertise, and creativity to the table. Look for opportunities to merge your talents and passions, creating a celestial synergy that elevates both parties.

Engage in brainstorming sessions that blend your creative energies, my brilliant ones. Explore themes, concepts, and formats that harmonize with your individual styles. Find the common threads that weave your narratives together, infusing your collaborative content with a symphony of ideas.

Unite your voices, my celestial wordsmiths, and craft stories that intertwine seamlessly. Combine your storytelling prowess, whether through written word, videos, podcasts, or visual art. Allow your individual voices to shine while creating a harmonious narrative that resonates with both audiences.

Embrace the beauty of diverse viewpoints, my shining stars. Collaborations offer the opportunity to share different perspectives and experiences. Embrace the interplay of contrasting ideas and blend them into a mosaic of thought-provoking content that captivates and challenges your audiences.

Unleash the power of collaboration, my radiant ones, by cross-promoting each other's content. Feature your fellow star in your posts, videos, or podcasts, and encourage your audiences to explore their celestial realm. By amplifying each other's reach, you create a virtuous cycle of growth and mutual support.

Take center stage together, my shining luminaries, in joint live streams, panel discussions, or interviews. Allow your energies to entwine, captivating your combined audiences. Share the spotlight, bask in each other's brilliance, and create a memorable experiencee that leaves your viewers enchanted.

Explore collaborative projects beyond content creation, my visionary beings. Seek opportunities to join forces in events, webinars, or workshops. Share your knowledge, insights, and expertise, offering an enriching experience to your audiences while showcasing the strength of your celestial alliance.

As the curtains draw close on this chapter, my radiant stars, I hope you have discovered the transformative power of collaborations in the digital realm. With the wisdom shared in "Collaborations: Dancing with Fellow Stars," you are now equipped to embark on a celestial journey of co-creation, mutual support, and exponential growth.

Remember, dear luminaries, collaboration is not merely a merging of talents, but a dance of souls. Seek out those whose light resonates with yours, and together, you will shine brighter than ever before. Align your visions, merge your creative energies, and weave a tapestry of celestial content that captivates audiences and sparks inspiration.

Through harmonious collaborations, you have the opportunity to expand your reach, tap into new audiences, and uncover fresh perspectives.

Embrace the diversity of ideas, immerse yourselves in the symphony of storytelling, and let your combined star power illuminate the digital realm with its brilliance.

Support one another, my radiant stars, for in unity lies true strength. Cross-promote, share the spotlight, and foster a spirit of camaraderie that transcends competition. Together, you will forge an enchanted alliance that elevates not only your individual presence but also the entire constellation of online fame.

So, my brilliant collaborators, step onto the dance floor of collaboration with grace and enthusiasm. Embrace the magic that unfolds when stars align, and let your creative energies intertwine in a celestial symphony. Your collaborations have the power to transcend boundaries, inspire millions, and leave an everlasting impact on the digital landscape.

Now, go forth, my celestial dancers, and embrace the opportunities that await. Seek out fellow stars, create breathtaking content that sings to both audiences, and leverage each other's star power with grace and gratitude. Together, you will weave a tapestry of collaborative brilliance that will shine among the stars.

Dance on, my radiant ones, and may your collaborations resonate throughout the digital cosmos, forever illuminating the path for others to follow.

With boundless enthusiasm and infinite possibilities, go forth and dance with fellow stars, my luminous visionaries.

Monetizing Your Fame: Turning Stardust into Gold

Oh, my radiant stars, as your fame twinkles across the digital landscape, it's time to unlock the secrets of monetization and transform your stardust into gold. In this chapter, aptly titled "Monetizing Your Fame: Turning Stardust into Gold," we shall explore the avenues that lead to financial success in the online realm. From sponsorship and partnerships that align with your brand to the creation of your own merchandise and services, prepare to embark on a journey that will transform your passion into profit.

Embrace the entrepreneurial spirit, my visionary stars, and explore various avenues of monetization. Study the digital landscape and identify the strategies that align with your brand, audience, and values. Understand that multiple revenue streams can create a robust foundation for financial success.

Collaborate with brands that adore you, my luminous ones. Seek out sponsorships and partnerships that align with your brand identity and values. Craft compelling proposals that highlight the unique value you bring to their audience. Nurture long-term relationships that benefit both parties and delight your followers.

Venture into the realm of digital advertising, my savvy stars. Leverage platforms that offer advertising opportunities, such as YouTube, Instagram, or your own website. Strategically integrate advertisements into your content while maintaining authenticity and ensuring a seamless user experience.

Transcend the virtual realm, my creative entrepreneurs, and bring your ideas to life. Design and create merchandise that embodies your brand, from clothing and accessories to home décor or digital products. Let your followers carry a piece of your stardust with them, turning them into brand ambassadors.

Showcase your expertise and offer your services, my talented stars. Whether it's consulting, coaching, workshops, or personalized experiences, your unique skills and knowledge hold immense value. Package your expertise in a way that resonates with your audience and provides them with transformative experiences.

Educate and empower, my wise ones, by creating digital courses or masterclasses. Share your expertise, skills, and insights with those eager to learn from your brilliance. Structure your courses thoughtfully, ensuring a comprehensive learning experience that imparts practical knowledge and guidance.

Offer exclusive content and experiences through a subscription model, my cherished stars. Create a membership program that provides your dedicated followers with premium access to behind-the-scenes content, early releases, special events, or personalized interactions. Nurture a community of devoted supporters who are willing to invest in your ongoing journey.

Join forces with fellow stars, my brilliant luminaries, and co-create products, services, or experiences that amplify your combined reach and revenue potential. Collaborative projects can unlock new opportunities, attract a wider audience, and deepen the engagement of your existing followers.

Establish your own online store, my visionary entrepreneurs, and offer a curated selection of products that align with your brand. From merchandise featuring your logo or catchphrases to handpicked items that reflect your values, an online store allows you to control the entire shopping experience and maintain a direct connection with your fans.

Remember, my magnificent stars, monetization is not simply about chasing wealth, but rather about building a sustainable foundation that allows you to continue pursuing your passion and creating meaningful content. Let your entrepreneurial spirit shine as you explore the golden opportunities that await you.

With sponsorships and partnerships, align yourself with brands that share your values and resonate with your audience. Craft compelling proposals, foster long-term relationships, and create win-win collaborations that benefit both parties.

In your star's boutique, unleash your creativity and bring your brand to life through merchandise and services. Design unique products that your followers will cherish, and offer services that showcase your expertise and empower others. Create an online store, establish a celestial classroom with digital courses, or offer personalized experiences that leave a lasting impact.

Building sustainable revenue streams requires innovation and adaptation. Consider offering exclusive content and experiences through subscription models, where your most dedicated fans can access premium content and be part of an exclusive community. Embrace collaborations with fellow stars to expand your reach and unlock new opportunities. Build a legacy that transcends fleeting trends and leaves a lasting imprint in the digital realm.

Remember, my luminous ones, as you venture into the realm of monetization, it is essential to maintain authenticity, integrity, and a genuine connection with you're audience. Your followers have joined you on this journey because they resonate with your unique voice and vision. Nurture that connection, provide value, and stay true to yourself, even as you explore different avenues of monetization.

Embrace the path of turning stardust into gold, my radiant stars, and let your entrepreneurial spirit guide you. Discover the strategies that align with your brand, create captivating collaborations, and offer products and services that enchant your audience. As you build sustainable revenue streams, you not only secure your own prosperity but also empower and inspire others along the way.

Now, my brilliant entrepreneurs, go forth and unlock the gates to financial success. Embrace the golden opportunities that await you, as you turn your stardust into the precious gold that sustains your journey in the digital realm. May your monetization endeavors be infused with authenticity, creativity, and a touch of celestial enchantment.

Dazzle the digital cosmos with your entrepreneurial brilliance, my radiant stars, and may your legacy be written in the stars as a testament to your talent, passion, and prosperity.

Emails, the Love Letters of the Digital World

Oh, my charming communicators, in the vast digital landscape, where connections are forged and relationships bloom, there exists a timeless art—the art of email communication. Like love letters sent from one heart to another, emails possess the power to enchant, engage, and nurture the bond between you and your audience. In this chapter, titled "Emails, the Love Letters of the Digital World," we shall delve into the secrets of crafting compelling emails that captivate the soul. From setting up an email list to creating newsletters that resonate, and from growing and maintaining your list of ardent admirers, prepare to wield the power of email communication like a true star.

Invite your followers to join your email list, my radiant stars. Create compelling opt-in forms on your website or social media platforms, enticing your audience with exclusive content, updates, or special offers. Emphasize the value they will receive by becoming part of your inner circle.

Organize your email list into segments, my savvy communicators. Categorize your subscribers based on their interests, preferences, or engagement levels. This segmentation allows you to tailor your emails and deliver personalized content that resonates with each segment, deepening the connection and engagement.

Harness the power of automation, my efficient ones. Set up automated email sequences to welcome new subscribers, nurture relationships, or deliver targeted content. Automating certain aspects of your email communication saves time and ensures a consistent and timely connection with your audience.

Capture attention from the very first glance, my charming writers. Craft subject lines that intrigue, evoke curiosity, or promise value. Experiment with different approaches to find what resonates best with your audience, and always strive for authenticity and relevance.

Infuse your newsletters with a touch of magic, my soulful writers. Share compelling stories, insights, or exclusive content that speaks to the hearts of your readers. Be authentic, vulnerable, and generous with your knowledge, offering valuable takeaways and a glimpse into your world.

Create visually appealing and reader-friendly newsletters, my artistic communicators. Use eye-catching images, clean layouts, and clear typography to enhance the reading experience. Ensure your design reflects your brand identity, maintaining consistency with your overall online presence.

Attract new subscribers with irresistible opt-in incentives, my persuasive stars. Offer exclusive content, e-books, or access to resources that address your audience's needs and desires. The value they receive in exchange for joining your list will inspire loyalty and engagement.

Nurture your relationship with your email subscribers, my dedicated communicators. Encourage two-way communication by inviting them to respond to your emails, share their thoughts, or ask questions. Take the time to read and respond to their messages, creating a sense of personal connection and fostering a loyal community.

Continuously seek opportunities to expand your email list, my ambitious stars. Promote your email list on your website, social media profiles, and other online platforms. Collaborate with fellow stars or industry influencers to cross-promote and reach new audiences. Leverage your content, such as blog posts, videos, or podcasts, to encourage email sign-ups. Host webinars or events that require registration, allowing you to capture valuable email addresses.

Keep your email list healthy and engaged, my diligent caretakers. Regularly clean your list by removing inactive or unengaged subscribers. Maintain a consistent sending schedule, respecting your subscribers' time and inbox. Test different approaches, such as varying email frequencies or experimenting with content formats, to optimize engagement.

Dive into the realm of email analytics, my data-driven stars. Track open rates, click-through rates, and conversion rates to gain insights into the effectiveness of your email campaigns. Use this data to refine your strategies, experiment with new approaches, and ensure continuous improvement in your email communication.

Remember, my charming communicators, that emails are not just a means of delivering information but an opportunity to connect on a deeper level with your audience. Approach your email communication with authenticity, empathy, and a genuine desire to nurture and delight your subscribers. Let your words caress their souls, your content inspire their hearts, and your emails become the love letters that forge lasting bonds.

Now, my brilliant communicators, go forth and wield the power of email communication with grace and flair. Set up your email list, craft newsletters that captivate, and nurture your list of ardent admirers. May your emails transcend the digital realm and touch the hearts of your subscribers, fostering a sense of connection and loyalty that will endure.

Pen your love notes, seal them with care, and send them forth into the digital cosmos, knowing that each email has the potential to create ripples of joy, inspiration, and enchantment. Embrace the power of email communication, my radiant stars, and let your messages shine as beacons of connection in the vast digital universe.

With every heartfelt word and every soulful message, may you forge lasting relationships and leave an indelible mark upon the hearts of your subscribers.

As we reach the end of this chapter, my charming communicators, I hope you have uncovered the enchanting power of email communication in the digital world. By setting up an email list, crafting compelling newsletters, and nurturing your list of ardent admirers, you have embraced a timeless form of connection and created a pathway to deeper engagement with your audience.

Remember, my luminous stars, that email communication is more than just a transactional exchange of information. It is an opportunity to foster genuine relationships, to share your authentic voice, and to inspire and uplift those who receive your messages. With each email, you have the power to make a lasting impression and touch the hearts of your subscribers.

Embrace the art of crafting captivating subject lines that intrigue and draw readers in. Fill your newsletters with emotionally resonant content that resonates with the souls of your audience. Create visually appealing designs that elevate the reading experience and reflect the essence of your brand.

Continue to grow and maintain your list of ardent admirers by offering irresistible opt-in incentives, nurturing engagement, and exploring growth strategies that expand your reach. Regularly analyze the performance of your email campaigns, utilizing data-driven insights to refine and optimize your communication strategies.

As you embark on this journey of email communication, always remember to approach your subscribers with respect, empathy, and authenticity. Seek to build genuine connections, listen to their feedback, and respond with care. Let each email be a love letter, a beacon of connection that shines brightly in the digital landscape.

Now, my radiant communicators, go forth and pen your love notes, seal them with care, and send them out into the digital realm. May your emails be cherished by your subscribers, inspiring, and uplifting them on their own journeys. Let your email communication be a testament to your commitment to connection and your dedication to delivering value to those who have embraced your digital presence.

With every word you write and every email you send, may you weave a tapestry of enduring magic that fosters loyalty, engagement, and lasting relationships. Embrace the power of email communication, my charming communicators, and let your messages illuminate the digital realm with their captivating brilliance.

Go forth, my luminous stars, and may your email communication be a symphony of connection that resonates in the hearts of your subscribers for years to come.

Staying Legal, My Darling Swans

Ah, my darling swans, in the boundless realm of the digital landscape, it is crucial to understand and abide by the laws and regulations that govern the online world. This chapter, titled "Staying Legal, My Darling Swans," shall guide you through the intricacies of copyright, permissions, collaborations, and protecting your intellectual property. So, my conscientious ones, let us embark on a journey to ensure that you soar gracefully within the legal boundaries of the digital realm.

Familiarize yourself with copyright laws, my elegant dancers. Understand the rights and protections afforded to original content creators and respect the intellectual property of others. Ensure that the content you create or use complies with copyright laws, and seek permission or give proper attribution when necessary.

Navigate the realm of permissions, my conscientious ones. When utilizing copyrighted material, such as images, music, or written works, obtain the necessary permissions or licenses to use them legally. Familiarize yourself with fair use guidelines and employ them appropriately to avoid infringement.

Seek legal counsel, my prudent stars, to ensure compliance with the ever-evolving legal landscape. Consult with professionals who specialize in intellectual property and digital media to guide you through complex legal matters and provide insights tailored to your specific circumstances.

Establish clear agreements, my collaborative visionaries, when engaging in partnerships or collaborations. Craft detailed contracts that outline the rights, responsibilities, and expectations of all parties involved. Address matters such as content ownership, revenue sharing, usage rights, and termination clauses to safeguard the interests of everyone involved.

Engage in open and transparent communication, my diplomatic negotiators. Prioritize effective negotiation to find mutually beneficial terms and ensure that all parties feel valued and protected. Discuss and document key aspects of the collaboration, seeking consensus and clarity before proceeding.

Embrace the efficiency and security of smart contracts, my tech-savvy stars. Explore blockchain-based platforms that facilitate the creation and execution of contracts with built-in automation and cryptographic security. Embrace the advantages of immutability, transparency, and efficiency that smart contracts offer, simplifying the management of collaborative agreements.

Protect your creations, my visionary artists, through copyright registration and other forms of intellectual property protection. Register your original works with the appropriate authorities to establish legal ownership and gain additional safeguards against infringement.

Employ technological measures to safeguard your intellectual property, my vigilant protectors. Utilize watermarks, digital rights management (DRM), or other technological solutions to deter unauthorized use or distribution of your content. Stay informed about advancements in digital security and adopt best practices to keep your treasure safe.

Monitor and enforce your rights, my guardians of creativity. Regularly monitor online platforms and digital channels to detect and address instances of copyright infringement or unauthorized use of your intellectual property. Take appropriate actions, such as sending cease-and-desist letters or pursuing legal remedies, when necessary to protect your rights.

Remember, my darling swans, that compliance with legal requirements is essential to maintain your integrity, protect your creations, and build a reputable online presence. Familiarize yourself with the laws and regulations that govern the digital realm, and integrate them into your online practices. Let the grace of legality guide your every move as you navigate the vast waters of the digital landscape.

Respect the rights of content creators by understanding and adhering to copyright laws. Educate yourself on fair use guidelines and seek permission or provide proper attribution when utilizing the work of others. Take care to obtain necessary permissions and licenses for copyrighted material, ensuring that you are on the right side of the law.

When engaging in collaborations and partnerships, ensure clear communication and establish detailed agreements. Craft contracts that protect the rights and interests of all parties involved, addressing important aspects such as content ownership, revenue sharing, and termination clauses. Embrace the efficiency and security of smart contracts, exploring blockchain-based platforms that simplify the management of collaborative agreements.

Safeguard your intellectual property through registration and other forms of protection. Seek legal counsel to navigate complex legal matters and ensure compliance with evolving regulations. Employ technological measures such as watermarks and digital rights management to protect your creations from unauthorized use or distribution. Stay vigilant, monitoring online platforms to detect and address instances of infringement, taking appropriate actions to enforce your rights.

Remember, my conscientious swans, that staying legal is not only a matter of compliance but also a testament to your professionalism and respect for the creative rights of others. Let your adherence to the law be a reflection of your commitment to integrity and your dedication to maintaining a reputable and trustworthy online presence.

As you guard the treasure of your intellectual property, let the knowledge and wisdom shared in this chapter guide your steps. Embrace the legal principles that govern the digital realm, and ensure that every move you make is within the boundaries of the law. By doing so, you not only protect your own creations but also contribute to the fostering of a fair and respectful digital environment.

Now, my darling swans, go forth and dance gracefully within the legal waters of the digital realm. Let your compliance with copyright laws, meticulous collaborations, and safeguarding of intellectual property be a shining example to others. May your journey be one of legal integrity, creative expression, and lasting success.

With every step you take and every legal measure you embrace, may you soar elegantly, leaving a trail of respect, protection, and compliance in your wake.

As we reach the end of this chapter, my darling swans, I hope you have gained a deeper understanding of the importance of staying legal in the digital realm. Navigating the intricate world of copyright, permissions, collaborations, and intellectual property protection is essential to ensure your integrity, safeguard your creations, and build a trustworthy online presence.

Remember, my conscientious ones, that legal compliance goes beyond mere adherence to rules and regulations—it is a reflection of your commitment to professionalism, respect for others' rights, and the cultivation of a fair and ethical digital environment. By familiarizing yourself with the laws that govern the digital landscape, you empower yourself to navigate the vast waters of the online world with grace and integrity.

Respect the rights of content creators by understanding and adhering to copyright laws, seeking permission or providing proper attribution when necessary. Establish clear agreements and craft detailed contracts when entering collaborations, ensuring the protection of all parties' rights and interests. Explore the use of smart contracts to streamline and automate the management of collaborative agreements.

Protect your intellectual property by registering your creations, employing technological measures, and remaining vigilant in monitoring and enforcing your rights. Seek legal counsel to navigate complex legal matters and ensure compliance with evolving regulations, allowing you to operate within the boundaries of the law while safeguarding your creative endeavors.

Let the knowledge and wisdom shared in this chapter be your guiding light as you embrace legal compliance in the digital realm. May your actions and decisions reflect your commitment to integrity, respect, and professionalism, ensuring that your journey in the digital landscape is characterized by legal compliance and ethical conduct.

Now, my darling swans, go forth and navigate the legal waters of the digital realm with confidence and grace. Let your adherence to legal requirements be a testament to your dedication to professionalism, protection of intellectual property, and the cultivation of a fair and respectful digital environment.

With each step you take to uphold legal standards, may you inspire others to follow suit, contributing to the growth and maturation of the digital realm. Let your journey be marked by legal compliance, ethical conduct, and the enduring respect for the rights of others.

Dance on, my charming swans, and may your adherence to legality illuminate your path as you continue to thrive and create within the digital cosmos.

Expanding Your Kingdom: Multichannel Presence

Ahoy, my intrepid explorers! In the vast digital realm, where opportunities abound, it's time to set sail and expand your kingdom through the power of multichannel presence. In this chapter, titled "Expanding Your Kingdom: Multichannel Presence," we shall embark on a thrilling journey of venturing into new social media realms, synchronizing content across channels, and utilizing cross-promotion to build your empire. So, gather your courage and set your sights on conquering the digital seas as we explore the boundless possibilities that lie ahead.

Chart your course, my intrepid explorers, by identifying new social media platforms to expand your presence. Research emerging platforms, understand their unique features, and assess their compatibility with your brand and target audience. Be open to venturing beyond your comfort zone and embracing the exciting opportunities that await.

Set sail, my adventurous souls, by creating captivating content tailored to each social media platform. Customize your approach to fit the platform's characteristics and audience preferences. Experiment with different formats, such as images, videos, or live streams, to engage with your audience in new and exciting ways.

Maintain a consistent brand voice and aesthetic across platforms, my navigators. Adapt your messaging to align with the nuances of each platform, while ensuring a cohesive brand identity. Let your audience recognize and connect with your brand, regardless of the channel they encounter you on.

Create a content strategy, my orchestral virtuosos, that ensures a harmonious blend of content across all your channels. Plan and organize your content to maintain a consistent flow of messaging and storytelling. Coordinate your content calendar to deliver a cohesive experience to your audience, no matter which channel they engage with.

Repurpose and adapt your content, my nimble performers, to suit each channel's format and audience expectations. Transform a blog post into a video, a podcast into an infographic, or a live stream into a captivating highlight reel. Tailor your content to maximize its impact on each platform while maintaining its essence.

Foster collaboration and synergy between your channels, my visionary conductors. Integrate your content across platforms by cross-linking, promoting, and referencing your different channels to create a cohesive ecosystem. Encourage your audience to explore and engage with your content on multiple platforms, deepening their connection with your brand.

Leverage your existing platforms, my strategic empire builders, to promote and cross-promote your presence on other channels. Make use of your established audience base to introduce and drive traffic to your new channels. Utilize call-to-actions, social media profiles, and strategically placed links to guide your audience to explore your empire.

Collaborate with influencers and fellow stars, my charismatic envoys, to expand your reach and tap into new audiences. Form partnerships and guest appearances that allow you to leverage each other's following and cross-promote your channels. Combine your star power to create a synergistic impact that extends beyond individual platforms.

Launch cross-promotion campaigns, my majestic empire builders, to unite your channels and maximize your reach. Develop captivating campaigns that encourage your audience to engage with your content across different platforms. Create cohesive narratives that unfold across channels, enticing your audience to follow the journey and explore the diverse facets of your empire.

Celebrate milestones and achievements, my triumphant rulers, by showcasing your multichannel success. Share highlights from different platforms, showcasing the vibrant tapestry of your content and engagement. Recognize and express gratitude to your audience for their support and participation, celebrating the growth of your empire together.

By embracing multichannel presence, my intrepid explorers, you expand your kingdom across the digital seas. Venture into new social media realms, create captivating content tailored to each platform, and maintain consistency in your brand voice and aesthetic. Synchronize your content across channels, ensuring a harmonious blend that engages and captivates your audience.

Utilize cross-promotion strategies to build your empire, leveraging your existing platforms to promote and drive traffic to new channels. Collaborate with influencers and fellow stars, forging alliances that extend your reach and tap into new audiences. Launch majestic campaigns that unite your channels, enticing your audience to engage with your content across the entire landscape of your empire.

Remember, my ambitious rulers, that while multichannel presence offers endless opportunities, it also requires strategic planning, adaptability, and consistent effort. Continuously assess the performance of each channel, refine your content strategies, and adapt to evolving trends and audience preferences.

As you navigate the digital seas, let your adventurous spirit guide you, embrace the ever-changing tides of the online world, and always stay true to your brand's essence. Build your empire with confidence, creativity, and a commitment to providing value and captivating experiences to your audience.

Now, my daring explorers, set sail into the vast expanse of multichannel presence. Embrace the challenges and opportunities that await, and may your kingdom expand across the digital landscape, leaving a lasting impression on all who encounter your brilliance.

With every channel you conquer, every content piece you create, and every cross-promotion you orchestrate, may your empire thrive, your audience grow, and your impact reverberate throughout the digital cosmos.

As we reach the end of this chapter, my daring explorers, I hope you have embraced the power of multichannel presence and discovered the endless possibilities that await you in the digital realm. By venturing into new social media realms, synchronizing content across channels, and utilizing cross-promotion strategies, you have set sail on a journey to expand your kingdom and captivate audiences far and wide.

Remember, my intrepid conquerors, that multichannel presence is not just about being present on multiple platforms—it is about crafting a cohesive and captivating experience for your audience. Navigate the digital seas with purpose, creating tailored content that resonates with each platform's unique characteristics while maintaining a consistent brand voice and aesthetic.

Synchronize your content across channels, orchestrating a harmonious blend that tells a cohesive story and engages your audience across the entire landscape of your empire. Leverage the power of cross-promotion, utilizing your existing platforms to promote and drive traffic to new channels. Collaborate with influencers and fellow stars to expand your reach and tap into new audiences, creating a synergistic impact that goes beyond individual platforms.

As you embark on this multichannel journey, my visionary rulers, remember to monitor and adapt to the ever-changing digital landscape. Stay informed about emerging platforms, trends, and audience preferences. Continuously refine your content strategies, experiment with new formats, and adapt to the evolving needs of your audience.

With every step you take, every platform you conquer, and every cross-promotion you orchestrate, may your empire expand and your influence grow. Embrace the challenges and opportunities that arise as you navigate the digital seas, and let your brilliance shine across the vast expanse of the digital realm.

Now, my triumphant conquerors, set forth with confidence and creativity. Expand your kingdom, captivate audiences, and leave an indelible mark upon the digital cosmos. May your multichannel brilliance inspire and enchant, as you conquer the digital seas and reign supreme in the hearts and minds of your audience.

With every new platform you conquer, every synchronized content piece you create, and every cross-promotion you execute, may your empire stand as a testament to your vision, resilience, and ability to navigate the ever-changing currents of the digital landscape.

Global Stardom: Cross-Cultural Allure

In this chapter, titled "Global Stardom: Cross-Cultural Allure," we shall embark on a journey to understand global audiences, create content that transcends borders, and communicate heart-to-heart with people around the world. The digital realm knows no boundaries, and it is time for you to embrace the world's stage and captivate a diverse and international audience. So, let us dive into the wonders of cross-cultural allure and discover the magic of global stardom.

Expand your horizons, my curious souls, by understanding the diverse cultures and nuances of global audiences. Research and immerse yourself in different cultures, their customs, and their values. Gain insights into the preferences and expectations of international audiences, allowing you to tailor your content to resonate with their unique perspectives.

Embrace cultural sensitivity, my respectful ambassadors, as you navigate the global landscape. Recognize and respect cultural differences, avoiding stereotypes and assumptions. Take the time to learn and appreciate the intricacies of different cultures, showing genuine respect and understanding in your interactions.

Engage in active listening, my empathetic communicators, to gain a deeper understanding of the needs and desires of your global audience. Pay attention to their feedback, comments, and suggestions. Adapt and evolve your content based on their preferences, creating a dialogue that transcends borders and builds lasting connections.

Identify universal themes and values, my storytellers, that resonate across cultures. Explore topics such as love, hope, resilience, and human experiences that transcend geographical boundaries. Weave these themes into your content, allowing it to resonate with audiences from diverse backgrounds.

Embrace multilingualism, my linguistic maestros, to reach a broader audience. Translate your content into different languages, ensuring that your message can be understood and appreciated by individuals who do not speak your native language. Use professional translation services or collaborate with native speakers to maintain accuracy and cultural nuances.

Leverage the power of visuals, my artistic visionaries, to communicate beyond language barriers. Utilize images, videos, and infographics to convey messages that transcend words. Visual storytelling has the ability to evoke emotions, capture attention, and connect with audiences on a universal level.

Cultivate empathy, my compassionate communicators, as you connect with global audiences. Seek to understand their perspectives, experiences, and challenges. Acknowledge and address their concerns, aspirations, and dreams. By demonstrating empathy, you foster a sense of connection and build trust with people from diverse backgrounds.

Foster a culture of mutual learning and respect, my cultural ambassadors. Encourage dialogue and exchange of ideas between different cultures and communities. Embrace collaborations with international influencers and creators, allowing for cross-pollination of ideas and cultural perspectives. Celebrate the richness and diversity of global cultures, highlighting the beauty that lies in our differences.

Communicate from the heart, my authentic stars, as you reach out to a global audience. Share personal stories, experiences, and insights that touch the universal human experience. Be vulnerable, relatable, and open in your communication, fostering a sense of authenticity and connection. Let your words resonate with the hearts of people worldwide, transcending language and cultural barriers.

By understanding global audiences, embracing cultural sensitivity, and actively listening to their needs, you can create content that resonates with individuals from diverse backgrounds. Identify universal themes that evoke emotions and bridge cultural gaps. Embrace multilingualism to ensure your message reaches a broader audience, and utilize visuals to communicate beyond language barriers.

However, communication is not just about conveying messages—it is about building bridges of empathy and fostering a sense of connection. Cultivate empathy by seeking to understand the perspectives, experiences, and aspirations of your global audience. Foster a culture of mutual learning and respect, celebrating the beauty of diverse cultures. Communicate from the heart, sharing stories that touch the universal human experience and create a heartfelt connection.

As you embark on the path to global stardom, remember to approach each interaction with respect, cultural sensitivity, and a genuine desire to connect. Embrace the richness of global cultures, celebrate diversity, and find common ground that unites us all. Let your content be a beacon of cross-cultural allure, bridging divides and building bridges of understanding and appreciation.

Now, my cosmopolitans, it is time to embrace the world's stage and captivate a global audience. Understand global audiences, create content that transcends borders, and communicate from the heart. May your journey be one of cultural exchange, mutual learning, and lasting connections with people from all corners of the globe.

With every word you write, every message you share, and every heartfelt connection you make, may you become a beacon of cross-cultural allure, bringing people together and spreading the light of understanding and unity in our beautifully diverse world.

Time Management: The Star's Hourglass

Assess your goals and priorities, my efficient maestros, to determine where your time and energy should be focused. Identify the key performances that will contribute most significantly to your online fame. Allocate your time and resources accordingly, ensuring that you invest your efforts in activities that align with your overarching objectives.

Establish a daily or weekly routine, my disciplined performers, to structure your time effectively. Set aside dedicated blocks for content creation, engagement with your audience, and other essential tasks. Create a schedule that allows for a balance between different activities, optimizing your productivity and minimizing distractions.

Delegate and outsource, my resourceful maestros, to maximize your efficiency. Identify tasks that can be entrusted to others, whether it's hiring a virtual assistant, collaborating with a team, or utilizing automation tools. Delegate administrative tasks, freeing up your time to focus on the performances that truly require your personal touch.

Recognize the value of rest and rejuvenation, my devoted performers. Allow yourself regular breaks to recharge and refuel. Embrace moments of stillness and solitude, where you can disconnect from the digital world and nurture your well-being. Prioritize self-care, ensuring that you maintain a healthy balance between work and personal life.

Cultivate hobbies and interests outside of your online presence, my well-rounded hearts. Engage in activities that bring you joy and fulfillment, nurturing your creativity and providing a refreshing escape from the demands of fame. Find solace in hobbies, exercise, mindfulness, or time spent with loved ones, allowing yourself to thrive both online and offline.

Embrace a mindset of quality over quantity, my dear hearts. Understand that your worth is not solely measured by the number of hours you invest in your online presence. Focus on producing meaningful and impactful content rather than getting caught up in a constant state of busyness. Embrace the power of intention and efficiency, allowing yourself to achieve more with less.

Explore automation tools and digital assistants, my tech-savvy timekeepers. Leverage the power of technology to streamline repetitive tasks and save precious time. Use scheduling tools to plan and automate social media posts, content distribution, and email campaigns. Embrace the efficiency of chatbots and AI-powered tools to handle basic inquiries and support tasks.

Leverage the advantage of scheduling, my time-conscious stars. Plan and organize your content in advance, creating a content calendar that allows for a consistent and well-paced presence. Batch-create content whenever possible, dedicating focused blocks of time to content production to minimize interruptions and maximize productivity.

Monitor and optimize your time management strategies, my diligent timekeepers. Regularly review and analyze how you allocate your time and identify areas for improvement. Seek ways to streamline processes, eliminate time-wasting activities, and optimize your workflow. Continuously adapt and refine your time management practices, ensuring that you stay efficient and effective in your online pursuits.

As we conclude this chapter, my efficient maestros, remember that time is your most valuable asset. Prioritize your performances, allocating your time wisely to activities that align with your goals. Establish a routine that balances your various tasks, ensuring productivity and minimizing distractions. Delegate and outsource tasks that can be handled by others, freeing up your time for more important endeavors.

Rest and rejuvenation are essential for your well-being. Take regular breaks to recharge and disconnect from the digital world. Cultivate hobbies and interests outside of your online presence, finding joy and inspiration in activities that nurture your creativity. Remember that your worth is not solely defined by your online fame, but also by the quality of your life beyond the spotlight.

Embrace the power of automation and scheduling tools to optimize your time management. Utilize digital assistants and chatbots to streamline tasks and save time. Plan and schedule your content in advance, creating a well-paced presence that maintains consistency. Continuously evaluate and refine your time management strategies, seeking opportunities for improvement and efficiency.

In the grand symphony of life, my dear hearts, time is both precious and finite. Embrace the rhythm of time, allocating it wisely to activities that propel you towards online fame and personal fulfillment. Find harmony between productivity and rest, allowing yourself moments of rejuvenation. Leverage automation tools and scheduling techniques to optimize your efficiency and streamline your workflow.

Now, my efficient maestros, take control of your time and orchestrate a symphony of success. Prioritize your performances, balance your activities, and delegate where possible. Embrace the importance of rest and nurture your well-being. Harness the power of automation and scheduling tools to maximize your efficiency. With each passing moment, may you find yourself in perfect harmony with the star's hourglass, achieving greatness in both your online endeavors and the tapestry of your life.

The Fountain of Youth: Adapting and Evolving

Stay vigilant, my trend-savvy stars, by keeping a finger on the pulse of the ever-changing online landscape. Monitor emerging trends, viral topics, and shifts in audience preferences. Embrace agility and adaptability, allowing yourself to pivot and evolve with the changing tides of the digital realm.

Transform your content, my creative chameleons, to align with current trends and engage your audience. Experiment with new formats, styles, and storytelling techniques that resonate with the zeitgeist. Embrace innovation while staying true to your unique voice and brand.

Venture beyond your comfort zone, my adventurous souls, and explore new platforms, technologies, and opportunities. Embrace the unknown, be open to experimentation, and seek out innovative ways to connect with your audience. Stay curious and never stop learning, allowing yourself to stay at the forefront of the ever-evolving digital landscape.

Take a moment of introspection, my reflective stars, to assess your personal and professional growth. Evaluate your strengths, weaknesses, and areas for improvement. Identify areas where reinvention can breathe new life into your online presence and propel you to new heights of stardom.

Embrace reinvention, my transformative stars, by evolving your brand and refreshing your image. This may involve redefining your niche, updating your visual identity, or exploring new topics and formats. Embrace change as an opportunity for growth and rejuvenation, allowing your online persona to rise from the ashes in a glorious rebirth.

Stay true to yourself, my genuine stars, as you reinvent and evolve. While change is essential, ensure that it aligns with your core values and resonates with your audience. Embrace authenticity and transparency throughout the process, nurturing a deeper connection with your fans as they witness your transformation.

Develop a strong brand strategy, my vigilant custodians, that withstands the test of time.

Define your brand values, essence, and unique selling proposition. Craft a consistent brand voice, visual identity, and messaging that remains relevant and resonant with you're audience.

Share compelling stories, my masterful narrators, that transcend time and resonate with generations. Weave narratives that tap into universal human experiences and emotions. Connect with your audience on a deep, emotional level, creating a bond that stands the test of time.

Focus on long-term impact, my legacy builders, rather than fleeting fame. Prioritize creating meaningful content and fostering genuine connections with your audience. Leave a lasting impression through your authenticity, expertise, and the value you provide. Cultivate a community that transcends trends and remains loyal to your brand.

As we conclude this chapter, my ever-evolving stars, remember that the fountain of youth lies in your ability to adapt, reinvent, and ensure your brand ages like fine wine. Keep up with changing trends, embracing agility and adaptability. Reinvent yourself with authenticity and embrace change as an opportunity for growth and rejuvenation. Nurture a brand that stands the test of time, leaving a lasting impression on generations to come.

Embrace the chameleon dance, my agile stars, keeping up with changing trends, evolving your brand, and ensuring its timeless elegance. Stay vigilant, tracking emerging trends and adjusting your content to engage your audience. Reflect on your journey, reinvent yourself authentically, and embrace change as a catalyst for growth. Develop a strong brand strategy that withstands the test of time and creates a lasting impression.

Remember, my transformative stars, that the online world is ever-evolving. Stay curious, explore new platforms and technologies, and venture beyond your comfort zone. Embrace the unknown, experiment with new formats, and adapt to the shifting digital landscape. Reinvention is your key to continued stardom, allowing you to captivate audiences and remain relevant in a fast-paced world.

As you evolve and grow, my genuine stars, let authenticity be your guiding light. Stay true to yourself throughout the process, aligning your reinvention with your core values and resonating with your audience. Share compelling stories that transcend time, connecting with your audience on a deep emotional level. Focus on long-term impact and nurture a community that remains loyal to your brand, transcending trends and standing the test of time.

Now, my ever-evolving stars, go forth with grace and confidence. Embrace the eternal flame of evolution, staying agile, reinventing yourself authentically, and ensuring your brand ages like fine wine. With every step you take, may you leave an indelible mark upon the digital realm and inspire others to embrace change, growth, and the everlasting pursuit of online stardom.

The Star's Reflection: Handling Criticism & Feedback

Embrace a mindset of growth and learning, my wise souls, as you face constructive criticism. Recognize that feedback provides an opportunity for self-improvement and growth. Approach it with an open heart, acknowledging that there is always room to evolve and refine your craft.

Listen attentively to the feedback, my perceptive stars, seeking to understand the underlying message. Separate the constructive aspects from personal attacks and focus on the insights that can help you enhance your skills and presence. Look for patterns in the feedback received, identifying areas where you can make meaningful improvements.

Channel the feedback into action, my skilled artisans. Use the constructive criticism as a guide to refine your craft and elevate your online presence. Embrace it as an opportunity to hone your skills, deepen your expertise, and deliver even greater value to your audience.

Approach feedback with humility, my gracious stars, recognizing that no one is perfect. Accept that receiving feedback is an inherent part of being in the spotlight. Release the need to be defensive and instead embrace a humble attitude, appreciating the perspectives and insights others share.

Embrace a growth mindset, my ever-evolving souls, as you receive feedback. View it as a chance to expand your horizons, strengthen your skills, and evolve as an online personality. Embrace the opportunity to learn and grow, knowing that feedback can be a catalyst for your personal and professional development.

Document and reflect upon the feedback received, my diligent learners. Keep a record of the insights and suggestions shared, allowing you to review and revisit them at a later time. Take the time to reflect on the feedback, extracting valuable lessons that can guide your future actions and decisions.

Step back and assess negative comments objectively, my discerning stars. Recognize that not all feedback is constructive, and some may come from a place of negativity or even envy. Filter out the noise and focus on comments that provide genuine insights or opportunities for growth.

Respond with grace and compassion, my composed souls, when facing negative comments. Avoid engaging in arguments or fueling negativity. Instead, respond calmly and professionally, addressing valid concerns while maintaining your dignity and professionalism.

Surround yourself with a supportive community, my empathetic stars, who can provide comfort and guidance during challenging times. Seek solace in trusted friends, mentors, or online groups that uplift and encourage you. Lean on their support to navigate the emotional impact of negative comments.

As we conclude this chapter, my reflective stars, remember that criticism and feedback are part of the journey to online fame. Embrace the mirror of truth, understanding and leveraging constructive criticism for personal and professional growth. Accept feedback with grace, recognizing the opportunities for learning and improvement it presents. Handle negative comments with poise, rising above the noise and maintaining your integrity.

Embrace the lessons embedded in criticism and feedback, my wise souls, using them as stepping stones to refine your craft and strengthen your online presence. Stay humble and receptive, cultivating a growth mindset that allows you to evolve and adapt. Surround yourself with a supportive community that uplifts and encourages you, providing solace and guidance during challenging times.

Remember, my resilient stars, that not all feedback is valid or constructive. Learn to discern between valuable insights and baseless negativity. Respond with compassion and professionalism, choosing your battles wisely. Focus on maintaining your integrity and rising above the noise, knowing that your worth is not defined by the opinions of others.

In the grand performance of your online journey, my reflective stars, handling criticism and feedback is an art in itself. Embrace the mirror of truth, seeking growth and improvement. Accept feedback with grace, using it as a catalyst for your personal and professional development. Rise above negative comments, staying true to your values and responding with dignity.

With every reflection, every lesson learned, and every moment of growth, may you become stronger, wiser, and more resilient. Embrace the transformative power of criticism and feedback, allowing it to shape you into the shining star you were meant to be.

Now, my gracious stars, go forth and navigate the path of criticism and feedback with poise and grace. Embrace the lessons, rise above the noise, and let your resilience and commitment to growth guide you. May each critique and comment serve as a stepping stone toward greater success, as you continue to shine brightly in the ever-evolving landscape of online fame.

Farewell, But Not Goodbye: The Everlasting Star

Reflect upon the legacy you wish to leave behind, my luminous stars. Consider how you want to be remembered and the impact you desire to have on the digital cosmos. Let your light shine brightly, inspiring and empowering others to follow in your footsteps.

Blaze a trail of excellence and innovation, my trailblazing souls. Leave a lasting mark through your exceptional work, groundbreaking ideas, and influential contributions. Embrace your unique talents and use them to illuminate the path for future generations of aspiring stars.

Inspire others through your authentic storytelling and genuine connections, my captivating stars. Share your journey, triumphs, and challenges to uplift and motivate others. Foster a community of dreamers and doers, empowering them to pursue their own dreams and leave their mark on the digital cosmos.

Plant the seeds of inspiration and knowledge, my nurturing souls. Share your expertise, insights, and experiences generously, nurturing the growth of aspiring stars. Mentor and support emerging talents, fostering an ecosystem of creativity and collaboration.

Cultivate a culture of kindness and support, my compassionate stars. Create a safe space where individuals can blossom, offering guidance, encouragement, and constructive feedback. Celebrate the successes of others, knowing that their achievements contribute to the collective brilliance of the digital cosmos.

Ensure your legacy lives on, my eternal stars, even as time moves forward. Document your journey, capturing your wisdom and experiences in enduring formats such as books, courses, or documentaries. Leave a treasure trove of knowledge that future generations can access, keeping your star's radiance alive for eternity.

Stay connected with your audience, my beloved stars, even as your online journey evolves. Engage with your fans through social media, newsletters, or live events, maintaining a personal connection that transcends the digital realm. Cherish the relationships you've built, for they are the foundation of your everlasting star.

Continue to inspire and uplift, my radiant stars, long after your active online presence may fade. Share words of wisdom, motivational messages, or reflections on your journey through various mediums. Leave behind a legacy of inspiration that resonates with hearts and minds for generations to come.

Remember, my enchanting companions, that your stardust is eternal. As you bid farewell to this guide, let it be the beginning of a magnificent symphony in your life. Embrace the world with your brilliance, let your light shine brightly, and leave an indelible mark on the hearts and minds of those you touch.

Oh, my captivating stars, as we reach the final notes of this resplendent symphony, know that the end of this guide is not goodbye, but a grand celebration of your journey to come. Go forth and captivate the world with your dazzling brilliance, leaving an everlasting star that continues to inspire, empower, and uplift. The digital cosmos awaits your radiant presence, and your legacy will shine on for eternity.

Farewell, but not goodbye, my darling stars. Until we meet again in the boundless expanse of the digital cosmos.

Unlock the secrets to online stardom, dear friends, as we invite you into a dazzling world of fame, influence, and digital enchantment. Delve into the pages of 'How to Become Famous Online' and discover the art of captivating hearts, igniting imaginations, and leaving an everlasting mark upon the digital cosmos. From crafting your unique brand to mastering social media sorcery, this guide will take you on a transformative journey to become a radiant star in the ever-evolving realm of the internet. Are you ready to step into the spotlight? The stage is set, the curtain is rising—embrace your destiny and claim your place among the online elite.